JUST ONE MESSAGE!

WRITTEN BY: DR. NAJI IBRAHIM

EDITED BY: ANN RONAYNE

In the Name of Allah, the Beneficent, the Merciful.

© Cooperative Office for Islamic Propagation in Rabwah , 2019

King Fahd National Library Cataloging-in-Publication Data

Ibrahim, Naji

Just One Message. / Naji Ibrahim .- Riyadh , 2019

88p ; 12 x 16.5 cm

ISBN: 978-603-8249-88-8

1-Islam - General Principles   I- Tile

210 dc   1441/3031

  L.D. no. 1441/3031

  ISBN: 978-603-8249-88-8

This publication is designed by Osoul Center. Permission is granted for it to be stored, transmitted, and published in any print, electronic, or other format - as long as the Osoul Center is clearly mentioned on all editions, no changes in the text are made without the express permission of the Osoul Center, and a high level of quality is maintained.

✉ P.O.BOX 29465 Riyadh 11457
@ osoul@rabwah.com
🌐 www.osoulcenter.com

To those who seek the truth sincerely,
honestly, and with an open mind!

Straight to the point

Since the creation of Adam, throughout history, just one original and eternal message has been delivered repeatedly to humankind.

To remind people of it and get them back on track, many prophets and messengers- including Adam, Noah, Abraham, Moses, Jesus, and Muhammad - were sent by the only True God to convey this message:

**THE TRUE GOD, THE CREATOR IS ONLY ONE.
WORSHIP HIM ALONE.**

JUST ONE MESSAGE!

THE TRUE GOD, THE CREATOR
sent these Prophets to convey this Message

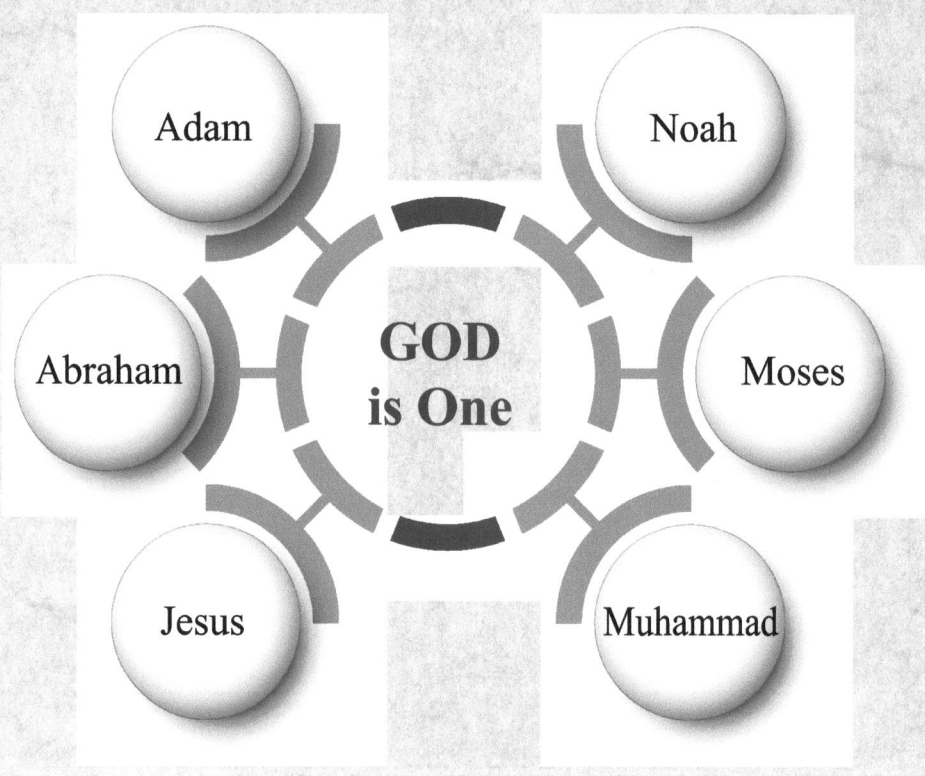

The One True God (Allah) sent these major prophets, as well as many other prophets and messengers, to accomplish various tasks and missions, some of which were:

1. To receive guidance from God and deliver it to their people.
2. To convey the message that God is One and to command their people to worship Him alone. (**NOT** to worship Brahma, Buddha, nature, Jesus, Muhammad, or any others!)
3. To be role models for their people.
4. To instruct their people to love and obey God, fear Him, and keep His commandments.
5. To teach their followers important religious and moral tenets and to advise them on worldly matters.
6. To guide those who had deviated, disobeyed God, or worshipped other false gods or idols.

7. To tell people about their final destination (the Last Day) and what will lead them to either Paradise or …

All those prophets and messengers were created and sent by the same God. He is the Creator of all humans, all animals, and all creatures and objects. It is this One True God (Allah) who created the whole universe, including nature and all it contains. He is the Creator of life, death, and life after death.

The Oneness of this True God, the Creator, can be easily found in the scriptures of the Jews, Christians, Muslims, and others.

By objectively studying the concept of God according to both the Bible and the Qur'an, a sincere seeker of the truth can easily discern the unique attributes belonging to the Only True God (Allah).

Some of the qualities that distinguish this Only True God from others who claim (or are claimed) to be God are:

- This True God is the Creator; He Himself is neither created nor born.
- The True God is *ONE*, not three or more! He has no partners or equals.
- This One True God (Allah) cannot be seen by humans in this life.
- The One True God (Allah) is not manifested or incarnated in any physical forms of His creation.
- This One True God (Allah) is eternal; He does not die or change.
- The One True God (Allah) is not in need of anyone, such as a mother, a wife, or a son; nor does He require food, drink, or any kind of help. It is others who need Him.
- This One True God (Allah) is unique in His attributes and qualities. No one is like

Him, and no human or animal descriptions can be attributed to Him.

We can use these criteria and qualities (as well as others belonging to Him alone) to evaluate any claim that someone or something is God.

Now let us turn to discussing the one message mentioned above, citing some of the Biblical and Qur'anic verses that confirm the Oneness of God (Allah). But before that, I would like to share with you this thought:

> **Some Christians might wonder, "It is obvious that God is One. We believe in One God. So what is the point?"**

After spending a great deal of time studying the Bible, reading various writings on Christianity and its history, and engaging in many dialogues with Christians, including church clergy, I have come to understand that most of them perceive this One God to include:

1. God the Father,
2. God the Son, and
3. God the Holy Spirit.

So, based on common sense and simple logic, a sincere and honest seeker of the truth might wonder:

- What do you mean by saying that GOD is ONE, while you refer to THREE GODS? (Does 1+1+1= 1?!)

- Is God ONE in THREE (1 in 3) or THREE in ONE (3 in 1)?!

In addition, according to Christian dogma (faith), these three 'Gods' have different identities, roles, and functions:

1. God the Father = *the Creator*

2. God the Son = *the Savior*

3. God the Holy Spirit = *the Counselor*

By the way, if Jesus, **'God the Son'** (or **'Son of God'**), were really God or part of the One God, wouldn't this contradict what the Bible itself reports?

You have never heard his voice or seen his face. (John 5: 37)

No one has ever seen him; no one can ever see him. (1 Timothy 6: 16)

I will not let you see my face, because no one can see me and stay alive. (Exodus 33: 20)

Based on these Biblical verses, I -with all due respect- sincerely and honestly ask: How can we reconcile the dogma that 'Jesus is God' with the Biblical testimony that *no one has ever seen God or heard His voice?!*

Didn't the people of his time, including his family and followers, **SEE** Jesus the **'God'** (or 'God the Son', as some Christians believe!) and **HEAR** his voice?

Is there any secret or hidden purpose concerning the truth about God?

In the Bible, God emphatically testifies:
"I am the Lord, and there is no other god. I have not spoken in secret or kept my purpose hidden... I am the Lord, and I speak the truth; I make known what is right." (Isaiah 45: 18-19)

So, what is the truth?

Now, let us take off on a journey to seek the truth about the One True God as described in the Bible and the Qur'an.

At the end of this journey, after your critical, sincere, honest, and thoughtful reading of

JUST ONE MESSAGE!

this booklet (and particularly the Biblical and Qur'anic verses cited below), please judge for yourself.

> TO BE AS OBJECTIVE AS POSSIBLE, I CITE THE VERSES WITHOUT ANY COMMENT. PLEASE READ THE FOLLOWING VERSES CAREFULLY AND CRITICALLY (WITHOUT ANY PRECONCEPTIONS).

The One True God in the Old Testament of the Bible

- *Listen, Israel! The LORD our God is the only true God!* (Deuteronomy 6:4)

- *How great you are, O Sovereign Lord! There is no one like you, and there is no God but you, as we have heard with our own ears.* (2 Samuel 7:22)

- *…So that you would know me and believe in me and understand that I am the only God. Besides me there is no other god; there never was and never will be. "I alone am the Lord, the only one who can save you.* (Isaiah 43: 10-11)

- *I am the first, the last, the only God; there is no other god but me.* (Isaiah 44: 6)

- *There is no other god. "Turn to me now and be saved, people all over the world! I am the only God there is. My promise is True, and it will not be changed. I solemnly promise by all that I am: Everyone will come and kneel before me.* (Isaiah 45: 21-23)

> **CAN YOU THINK OF OTHER SIMILAR ONES?**

The One True God in the New Testament of the Bible

- *And, behold, one came and said unto him (Jesus), Good Master, what good thing shall I do, that I may have eternal life? And he (Jesus) said unto him, Why callest thou me good? there is none good but one, that is, God: but if thou wilt enter into life, keep the commandments.* (Matthew 19: 16-17)

- *And eternal life means to know you, the only True God, and to know Jesus Christ, whom you sent.* (John 17: 3)

- *Worship the Lord your God and serve only him!* (Matthew 4: 10)

- *Hear, Israel! The Lord our God is the only Lord.* (Mark 12: 29)

22 JUST ONE MESSAGE!

- ***For there is one God, and there is one who brings God and human beings together, the man Christ Jesus.*** (1 Timothy 2: 5)

CAN YOU RECALL OTHER VERSES CONFIRMING THAT GOD IS ONLY ONE? **(NOT THREE!)**

The One True God (Allah) in the Glorious Qur'an

- *Say, "He is Allah, [who is] One, Allah, the Eternal Refuge. He neither begets nor is born, nor is there to Him any equivalent."* (112: 1-4)

- *"There is no deity except Me, so worship Me."* (21: 25)

- *That is Allah, your Lord; there is no deity except Him, the Creator of all things, so worship Him. And He is Disposer of all things.* (6: 102)

- *Indeed, your God is One.* (37: 4)

- *And your god is one God. There is no deity [worthy of worship] except Him, the Entirely Merciful, the Especially Merciful.* (2:163)

THIS MESSAGE CONCERNING THE **ONENESS OF GOD** (IN ARABIC, *TAWHEED*) IS THE *ESSENTIAL THEME OF THE QUR'AN.*

Conclusions

These verses, as well as hundreds of similar pieces of evidence in the Bible and the Qur'an, confirm this one eternal message: that the True God is only ONE. *"Turn to me now and be saved, people all over the world! I AM THE ONLY GOD THERE IS."* (Isaiah 45: 22)

Not only does the Bible affirm that God is only ONE, but it also reveals that the True God, the Creator, is **the only Savior**. *"I am the only God. Besides me there is no other god; there never was and never will be. I alone am the Lord, the only one who can save you."* (Isaiah 43:10-11)

According to this affirmation, all other supposed gods or deities like Jesus, the Holy Spirit, Brahma, Vishnu, Shiva, Krishna, or Buddha are neither gods nor manifestations of the ONE True God.

To sum up, all God's prophets and messengers - including Adam, Noah, Abraham, Moses, Jesus, and Muhammad - were sent by the same God, the Creator, to convey the same message:

THE TRUE GOD, THE CREATOR IS ONLY ONE.
WORSHIP HIM ALONE.

Since these prophets and messengers all preached the same message, their religion must be the same! So what is the religion of these prophets and messengers of God (Allah)?

Submission to the will of God is the essence of their message. This word 'SUBMISSION' is the meaning of the Arabic word 'ISLAM'.

The Qur'an does confirm that 'Islam' is the True religion of all God's prophets and messengers. This Qur'anic fact is also found in the Bible itself!

"Submit yourselves therefore to God." (James 4:7)

Ultimately, to attain salvation, we must receive and believe in the above-mentioned message willingly and wholeheartedly. But this is not enough! We must also believe in all God's True prophets and messengers (including Prophet Muhammad) and follow their True guidance and teachings. **This is the gateway to a happy, eternal life!**

If you are a sincere seeker of truth and salvation, you should consider this **NOW**, before it is too late! **BEFORE DEATH! It could be soon! Who knows?**

One more thing…

A final thought!

> If you are sincere, honest, serious, objective, and open-minded in seeking the truth, then after thinking critically about this one message, you may be asking questions like:

√ So, what is the truth?

√ What can I do now?

If you sincerely believe in your only True God (Allah) and in His Last Prophet Muhammad, then **YOU CAN** pronounce the following:

"I testify that there is no god but Allah, and I testify that Muhammad is the messenger of Allah."

In Arabic, it reads:

which sounds like this:

ASH-HADU ALLA ILAHA ILLA ALLAH, WA ASH-HADU ANNA MUHAMMADAN RASOOLU ALLAH.

This is the testimony of faith and the gateway to Islam that one needs to utter in order to embrace Islam.

Yes, you can do it!

This testimony is your first step on the way to eternal life and is also your real key to the gate of Paradise.

If you decide to take this path, you can contact a Muslim friend, visit the suggested websites at the end of this booklet, visit the nearest Islamic center, or e-mail us at:

info@discoveritsbeauty.com

Basic Islamic Names and Terms

Allah: in Arabic, Allah is the proper name of the One True God, the Creator. Islam teaches that Allah is the True God of all humankind. Jewish and Christian Arabs use this name (Allah) to refer to God, and it is the word used for God in Arabic-language Bibles.

Muhammad (may Allah's blessings and peace be upon him): the last Prophet of the One True God (Allah); sent to all humankind.

Islam: submission to the Will of the One True God (Allah), the Creator.

Muslim: one who submits to the Will of the One True God (Allah).

The Glorious Qur'an: the final Word of the One True God (Allah), as revealed to Prophet Muhammad.

Are You Curious?

If you are curious and interested in discovering more information about Islam, please visit our website:

www.discoveritsbeauty.com

Feel free to e-mail your questions or feedback to:

info@discoveritsbeauty.com

Writings by the Author

- Just One Message!
- God in Christianity… What is His Nature?
- Have You Discovered Its Beauty?
- 100 Tweets About Islam
- 50 Tweets About Oneness of God
- 100 Short Phrases about Muhammad
- The Series 'Discover Its Beauty in 7 Minutes' (Newly Developed!):

  1. Just the Tip of the Iceberg
  2. The Religion of Adam and Eve
  3. The ABCs of Islam
  4. Answering Humanity's Critical Questions
  5. His Beautiful Names
  6. The Last Revelation
  7. The Final Messenger

Useful Islamic Websites

http://www.allahsquran.com

http://www.quranexplorer.com

http://www.islamhouse.com

http://www.edialogue.org

http://www.islamreligion.com

http://www.newmuslimguide.com

http://www.aboutislam.chat

http://www.guidetoislam.com/en/

Since the creation of Adam, throughout history, just one original and eternal message has been delivered repeatedly to humankind. Many prophets and messengers ﷺ including Adam, Noah, Abraham, Moses, Jesus, and Muhammad ﷺ were sent by the only True God to convey this message:

The True God, The Creator, Is Only ONE. Worship Him Alone

JUST ONE MESSAGE!
The True God, the Creator is only **ONE**.
Worship Him **ALONE**.

www.ingramcontent.com/pod-product-compliance
Lightning Source LLC
LaVergne TN
LVHW070438080526
838202LV00038B/2843